The
Chastening
of
Narcissus

HAROLD GRIER McCURDY

The
Chastening
of
Narcissus

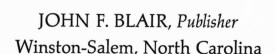

JOHN F. BLAIR, *Publisher*
Winston-Salem, North Carolina

To

William Wallace Davidson

Editor, *The Georgia Review*, 1957–68

namque tu solebas
Meas esse aliquid putare nugas

We plow in stubborn clay a crooked furrow,
We Southerners, and border the sad land
With sassafras, not olive trees or laurel:
But far off, in blue haze, magnolias stand.

Contents

Acknowledgments

Versions of some of the poems in this volume have been published before: "Lizard," in *The Scientific Monthly*; "The Transmigrant," in *New Directions in Prose and Poetry*, No. 11; "Fifty Couplets on an Old Romance," "Orton Plantation," "I Stepped Out," "Lost," "At Nobska," "There Where I Have Not Come," "Michelangelo, Old, with a Symbol of the Redeemer," in *The Georgia Review*. Four of the *Georgia Review* poems appeared in anthologies published by Borestone Mountain Poetry Awards. I thank the several publishers for permission to reprint. I also thank Mr. Frank Magro, literary executor of Sir Osbert Sitwell, for permission to use the quotation at the head of "The Far East," under the original date but slightly modified to conform to the text in *Pound Wise*, Little, Brown & Co., 1963.

NARCISSUS

You have seen, Narcissus, in the unflecked water
Your own pure body more beautiful than clouds
Your eyes more beautiful than any flowers.

Now at the fall of evening when the ebbing sunlight
Flows weakly back under the earth's edge
And the stars are not yet out, nor the moon up,

What are you in the dew-chill but a pale shadow
Blurring the dark shadow of water, a seen
Remembrance of the nymph's voice calling?

Were you afraid of the earth-smell clinging to her,
Were you afraid of the grass-stained flanks, the hands
Smelling of crushed leaves and the gathering of wild grapes?

The clear voice of her that flowed over you as the water
Flows over your image (and the image remains):
You were not afraid of this, you were afraid of

The darkness between her thighs and the menacing flowers
Upon her breasts like pale open roses: suggesting roots
Going deep in the earth and the eventual darkness

Deeper than sleep or love, the swallowing shadow
That the earth throws over all those who love the earth,
That goes as far as to the stars even, and eclipses
The pale shell of the moon.

December 20, 1934
Salisbury

THE ROSE

Inextricably through gnarled
Roots and receptive leaves
Sunlight and rain are snarled
Into the rose time weaves,
Into the sweet, sweet rose,
The difficult sweet rose
Not every day achieves.

One rose I snatch and fling
At infinity's mute face.
Does the petulant challenge sting?
Does a fire suffuse the place
Where a rose, my rose, this rose,
This difficult sweet rose
Struck with its burden of days?

April 2, 1936
Durham

3

IN THE CITY

Under the built buildings and the building
(Racket of rivets) walks the casual wind,
Fingering cigarette stubs, and smoke, and the thinned
Vocables of desire. (Where are the eagles, tilting
Over the rocks and balsams? Where is the wonder
Of a girl's hair shining on stricken eyes?)
The wind, triangular between her thighs,
Flickers the burning lids, and the words blunder
(Green lights along the main stem, Alysoun!)
But not the eyes: the eyes bore straight ahead.
("At puberty, I tied my breasts down; and when I bled,
I was frightened.")
                    In the violent noon
He landed, gliding. Climbed from the cockpit. Scotched her.
"A honey! Sweetest thing to handle you ever touched."

September 4, 1936
Durham

4

ANSCHLUSS

Here now in these last days the last of us
Fight for the memory of a precious thing,
Turning against the guns and armored fuss
The opening flowers of this final spring.
White, yellow, pink, and burning rose they burst
Lively among the leaf-flare everywhere,
Lively and soon, before the world is hearsed
In rattling iron and draped in black despair.
Now every man among us who can hear
The twittering birds and roaring winds of March,
And gathers to his soul the tender, dear,
First flowers of this spring, constructs his arch
Triumphal and memorial, and sets fire
To every fear that checked his heart's desire.

March 14, 1938
Durham

THE REVENANT

On Golgotha the hollow skulls are mold;
Beneath the long grass under the still sky
Victim and executioner are cold.

But there are places where the wind will sigh,
Shadowy places, violet-scented woods,
And windless places, hot and bright and dry,

Blanched and sun-hammered, burning solitudes,
Where even at noon a sorrowful ghost appears
To vex the wayfarer who halts and broods,

Tissued of nothing, if not blood and tears,
And like no man, if not one crucified,
Coming with groaning and the clash of spears.

He, who hourly a thousand deaths has died
Since Jew and Roman took each other's part
And Simon, called the Rock, trembled and lied,

Still walks in the dark mind, the barren heart,
With quick and anxious pace. The vault of space
Is crowded with his presence. Science and art

Are equally his, and his the munitions base
Where men store up the thunders of their wrath,
His the burst guts, the pain, the bleeding face,

And his the lull, the peace, the aftermath,
The fractured windows jewelling a crown,
The lonely step upon the cloistered path.

O monasteries, O silent white and brown
Mountains and fallow fields, where morning brings
The open light unbearable, gliding down

On hawk-and-eagle-shouldered outstretched wings,
Commend us all to Christ, the human Lord!
We cannot bear much thinking on these things.

Commend us all to Christ, lest at a word,
Unwitting, or by music startled, we,
From playing at our cards, or trade, or sword,

Turn, and look up, and hard behind us see
That terrible and immortal Sufferer spread
Cross-wise above the world, that agony

Blotting the known things out in gray and red . . .

March 24, 1940
Johnson City

THE FAR EAST

"Slowly, painfully, the old men hobbled along the crooked, paved paths that zig-zagged to these trees. . . . Once there, they would remain a full hour, matching in their minds the complexion and fragrance of the blossom of previous years with that before them."—Osbert Sitwell, "Old Worlds for New," *Life and Letters Today*, April 1942.

I see before my eyes
Those wrinkled gentlemen
So disciplined and so wise
Paying their dues again
(As spring after spring they do)
From temple step and tower
To the long opulent view
Of an orchard in full flower.

They too, as well as we,
Have felt the shocks of time
Disturb the serenity
Which neither rite nor rhyme
Nor poppied sleep nor love
For all its vaunted power
Can keep for us, above
One brief sweet fragile hour.

Long before gunboat or bomb
Was launched by violent hands
In the name of Christendom
Against those heathen lands,
Chinese and Japanese,
Their earth belched thunder and fire
And brought them to their knees
As low as God could desire.

Patience they have learned,
Patience and discipline,
And patiently some have returned
To gather brief beauty in,
Standing by one and two
Under the blue-tiled tower
For a long opulent view
Of an orchard in full flower.

May 18, 1942
Raleigh

ORION

Bright-belted Orion looked through our windows
(Who had looked through the windows of Rome,
And, ages before that, through the cave's mouth
At neolithic Venus and beetle-browed Apollo),
Bright-belted Orion looked through our windows
And saw our little boy sleeping and dreaming
Of hideous carnivorous lions always defeated
By kindly Dog and Pussy and Chipmunk,
And, seeing him so (so young, tender, and valiant),
Got new courage for his own old battle
With the red-eyed Bull that rages in heaven.

November 18, 1944
Raleigh

LOMBARDY

Arching over the rigid roof, the poplar,
Dark, a dark wave, twinkling, gesticulating,
A wave, or a dolphin's back, oiled, slick-rippling,
Leaps, restless, past the unmoving roof-edge,
Heady tumult of time at the margins of Euclid.
Light is squared and flattened along the windows;
Shallow, is cubed and edged by the fraudulent clapboards:
Tenuous planes, flat scapulas, bones enclosing
(Hollow, frailer than egg-shell, dark doom upon it)
Nothing: as in a sepulchre, where no ghost going
Wanly illuminates the dust of nothing.
The rippling dark-arched wave of the flowing poplar
Points beyond to the bluing headland, the sculptured
thunder,
There where the combed-wool hulking cloud-bank plunges
Dumbly its blunt nose in the silent azure . . .
Evening gathers inscrutable edgeless power.

May 17, 1945
Raleigh

THE TRANSMIGRANT

Between waking and sleeping, in that land
Neither ours nor theirs, where the keyhole
Lets in a dusty streamer of light, illuminating
A hoof or a fin or the half-face of a stranger,
Between rational and irrational, I saw
Clerkly Pythagoras, who, stunned by the surge of numbers
Rolling their dice along the resonant shore,
Meditated upon the permutations of his body,
That sieve and whirlwind like a twanging cord
Musical between the sharp horns of a triangle.
The bossed shield of Euphorbus clanged in his thought
Against the gold breastpin of Helen, and towers
Fell with a crash of china cups and saucers, or flared
Suddenly up and out like a newspaper
In the swift draft of a furnace. And he was there
Caught in the crisscross of bony fingers of light,
Among the guttering candles and glories of time,
Cobwebs and rotten rafters and old iron,
Eternally growing, like a cellar plant,
Pale, thin and limber, and too full of juice;
Eternally growing, whether he would or no,

Among the scrap iron and scrap lumber of history,
Weak as a hydrocephalic touched by the sun's last rays,
Pale plant in a cracked pot. "My life is weary," he said,
"And neither the iceman cometh, nor the hot Saviour
Making a crossmark beautiful on the night sky,
Flying and singing like a fiery swan.
I am St. Ixion on the turning wheel,
Tantalus between the cup and the grape,
Neither Christian nor Dionysian. Limbo is my home.
My ears are stuffed with the unbaptized crying
Of babes born out of wedlock. I cannot hear
Any new thing, nor experience a revelation
Through the cataracts of my eyes. My one talent
Corrodes in its burial hole, peevish with age,
Thin tentative creeper of the chlorotic soul,
Anaemic and amnesic; and the cord twangs
Irrational on the horns of the moon; the hypotenuse
I cannot measure, cannot gamble away."
The dicing numbers sobbed and sobbed on the shore,
And, mixed with that sobbing like a crooked smoke,
The emanations of his powerful mind

Rose fatly on my dream, and scented the cave
(Where in the dark the Platonic sleepers lie)
With an odor like violets, or
The burnt letters of a lost love.

May 30, 1945
Raleigh

THE FIELD

Something's astir in me. Is it a sparrow that perches
Alert on a swinging wire to deliver a pebbly trill,
Along the burdocky field's edge, above the twinkling
    birches,
Near its nest in the plum bush, under the clean-plowed hill?

Is it a pink-billed field sparrow? And is there a rusty wire
Swinging somewhere inside me, blessed by its tiny feet,
Where the wind gets under its feathers and its blood surges
    up in desire,
And its song spills over, is scattered, is suddenly awkward
    and sweet?

I have been proud and silent, shut mouth and love up,
    darling,
Up in an idiot silence, when you were familiar and near.
I pay in tears for that folly; and think how the winds will be
    hurling
The yellow leaves from the birches at the ruined end of the
    year,

And nowhere a perch for the sparrow, no singing at all then,
   but only
The sighing of withered grasses under the bush and the wire,
And the yellow dank leaves settling, and all that region
   lonely
Where now the field sparrow sings, dear, the blossom is
   white on the brier.

June 17, 1946
Raleigh

FIFTY COUPLETS ON AN OLD ROMANCE

"La princesse dans un palais de rose pure"—Valéry

I.

A swarm of gnats danced in a dappled lane
Long hours of afternoon, and drops of rain
In sudden handfuls dashed the summer flowers,
Brilliant with sunlight. Clouds like fairy towers
Mushroomed into the sky's exalted blue.
Upon that scene a horse of milky hue,
With azure trappings, tinkling silver bells,
Trotted on delicate hooves like a gazelle's;
And, on his back, a youth most fair of face.
A horrible hedge of thorns ran by the place,
Thick as a stormy midnight. Bones were strewn,
And rusty armor, dinted like the moon
Bewitched and lost, and long-unsounded horns,
In lewd abandon under those dark thorns.
There, with a spilling melody of bells,
The horse, on delicate hooves like a gazelle's,
Toward the hedge turned, and, lightly stepping over
The inoffensive skulls like heads of clover,
Entered a secret path not seen before;
Or maybe it was that radiant youth he bore

Who by a jubilant blowing on his horn
Relaxed the growth, and parted thorn from thorn.

II.

Five centuries of barbed and bitter shade
Let them at last into a park or glade
Where jets of water arching from carved stone
Stood motionless as stonework, and birds flown
Halfway from branch to branch in middle air
Had stopped, unfalling, as if painted there.
Unfluttering butterflies with reaching tongue
Above perpetual spikes and umbels hung.
Red carp were fixed astonished in their ponds.
A dial shielded with its thumb of bronze
An unevaporating dewy wedge
Of matin coolness ancient as the hedge.
Lightly indeed the horse and rider moved:
No hoofprint on the grass their passage proved,
No creak of saddle-leather, no bell-sound,
Nor stir nor echo from the trees around.
It was a vacuum world in which was no
Movement except their movement. Even so
We look at pictures, Greek or Byzantine,

Giotto's or Tintoretto's, and the scene
That grew from life and under a live hand
Invites us onward, but the silent land
Is silent, and repels the faintest trace
Of us or ours. So that horse's pace
Was far more delicate than a gazelle's,
And silent the small clamor of those bells
That hung like tears along the azure rein,
And silence reigned within the rider's brain.

III.

The princess, in a palace of pure rose
Set on a hill within a garden close
Among trim shrubs clipped into tortured shapes
And coiling vines with clusters of green grapes,
Slept without breathing, and yet seemed to sigh,
Fluent from pillowed head to languid thigh
And the small-ankled foot; light as a leaf
Or Botticelli's Flora fallen in grief.
A green diaphanous veil of fragrant lawn
Revealed, as by a sensitive pencil drawn,
The ambuscaded mysteries of the flesh,
Unique pale-gold, and frail, and virgin-fresh.

Over the sculptured beauty of her sleep
Baroque lacework of shadows, morning-deep,
Was from a tendrilled casement softly spread
In indiscreet delight from foot to head.
Across those shadows fell one shadow more
That moved, and reappeared inside the door,
Borne on those delicate hooves like a gazelle's
To the accompaniment of unheard bells;
And the fair youth looked in upon his dream.

IV.

Life's stillness, not its motion, is our theme.
How, then, describe with truth the fated kiss
Which woke from abnegation into bliss
The sorrowful sleeper, and whose motion stirred
Five hundred motionless years, released the bird
Painted in air between jade branch and branch,
Clove stone from water, let the red carp launch
Subaqueous fights and loves, the butterfly
Settle upon its flower, and the eye
Of the gold sun dry up the ancient dew
Behind the gnomon? How can words be true?
Or how can truth that is abstract and still

Enter into the fleshed and moving will?
That horse whose delicate hooves were a gazelle's
Whinnied upon the threshold, and the bells
Tinkled aloud, a silver laughing speech,
While the fair youth and princess each on each
Bent wondering eyes, and for an eternal hour
Lived in each other's gaze as wind in flower.

V.

Adventure is the essence of our ways,
The folly and nobility of our days.
Shall we not let these fortunate lovers go
(Perish the rose palace and black hedge-row!)
Out from the lethargy of magic boughs
Into the troubled world, and by sweet vows
Govern it to their going?
                                        Departing bells
Tink in the ear, the light hooves of gazelles
Patter on fallen leaves. A fury of rain
Scatters the gnat-swarm in the darkening lane.

July 5–6, 1946
Raleigh

DITHYRAMB

Odor of living sweat, warm neighborhood
Of the immediate body, closer than roses
Pendent and glowing, closer than stars
(Though nothing inanimate is closer than these
Ancient companions of love) . . .
       I seize
Aphrodite by the long gold daylight of her hair,
Am borne out on the long waves of it beyond myself,
Ferried upon the animal emanations of her flesh,
Toward the inexhaustible real, creation's seed-bed,
Where the unborn gods are a twilight within twilight,
A tremor of blueness in the blackberry blueness of midnight,
Back to the beginning, which is
Water, said Thales,
Air, said Anaximenes,
But boundless, boundless, murmured Anaximander.

July 10, 1946
Raleigh

ORTON PLANTATION

Gnarled graybeard oaks; and, through the long beards
   drifting,
The noonday light sunken to twilight values,
Clouded by weary lichens, blown and shifting.

The gravel path was edged by fiery camellias,
By banana-sweet magnolias; and, descending,
Flamed suddenly out on turns with massed azaleas.

Here that imported glory comes to an ending.
He called himself a king, the river planter
Whose brick-and-mortar tomb, flaking and blending

Into the marsh, far from the garden's center,
Squats here, a dim moon-ghost at noon, disdaining
The buglike fiddler crabs that round it canter.

A spirit more of tiredness than complaining
Saturates and surrounds it, weird and barren;
An atmosphere, as if forever raining.

Though other tombs wear lily or rose-of-Sharon,
Here only gnarled gray oaks, the strange light sifting,
Clamor and groan of alligator and heron.

July 14, 1946
Raleigh

THE STILL SEASON

Music has fallen, from the high branch has fallen,
Into the grass;
Cricket and grasshopper slowly, slowly,
Chant the earth's mass.
At night there's a thin piping, as southing
The birds pass.

Pride has forsaken us, pride has forsaken
The shame-colored leaves;
The tall corn is shocked, the mouse and the rabbit
House in the sheaves.
In the frayed marsh-grass and the cattails
The wind grieves.

For consolation, the late scattered flowers,
Liatris, aster,
Coiled morning-glories pale on the bean-poles.
But the heart's disaster
Is plain, is written in blood on the dogwood;
And slain is the Master.

October 6, 1946
Raleigh

SCENE

At the window, her white curtains,
Motionless, but feathering the light,
Travel toward evening, toward the dark east and the stars,
Lifting their ruffles (O white goshawk
Which her fist released!) as if the wind
Flowed, and their delicate tissue
Drank the advancing shadow.

Her blue parasol depends from a glass knob,
Her white gloves lie crumpled upon the table.

October 22, 1946
Raleigh

MINUET

Continually the light plays through the leaves,
As if the light were moving in a dance,
As if the light were dancing with the leaves.

So intertwisted in their love they are,
The quick and reaching tree, the spilling light,
Their marriage is complete, no doubt deflects.

Their motion is my rest. To see them move
Renews me like a fountain, rising, falling.
I rise and fall with them, I share their love.

And this is real, no dream. The universe
Is concentrated here, in this fact lives,
Today, in daylight, at green summer's verge.

June 16, 1947
Raleigh

FOCUS

Upon one focus we live.
The sun, or, dim in shrine,
Some image fugitive
From vulgar touch, is divine.

But not because common, nor
Because unique and hid,
Does image or sun count more
Than the roof over one's head.

Its preciousness comes about
From being in fact the center,
The final sure redoubt
No enemy can enter.

Outward the self expands
Its sphere of influence,
Draws chattels, house, and lands
Within its circumference,

Demands the universe.
Defeated, frightened at last,
Retreats, crying for mercy,
And finds the forgotten guest —

Ra, or Apollo, say,
Or, by some private name,
Hearth-fire or star whose ray
Counters the threatening gloom.

So Socrates at the end,
Not noted for pious fraud,
A skeptic mind did bend
To hymn a primitive god;

Admitted that in his ears
The mystic illogical flute
Hummed louder than his fears
And terminated dispute.

May 9, 1948
Raleigh

A MOBILE

Wire and string
Comprise the thing:

Wire for bone
Of the skeleton,

String to serve
For the fine nerve.

More bodiliness
It scorns as excess.

String taut
With intense thought,

Wire bright
With abstract light,

It swings, swings,
In intelligent rings;

A species of grace
Vibrant in space.

November 12, 1949
Chapel Hill

LIBATION

Let grape's blood stain the water, where the leaves,
Already stained by autumn, matted lie,
And, hidden underneath them, cold and shy,
The dusky salamander slightly heaves.

Your young hand on the cleft rock where you lean
To pour the curling wine's inverted smoke
Is warmer than the sun's diminished stroke
Broken across the branches' ragged screen,

Though, like your hand, which love instructs, your heart
Warms the denuded year. Empty the bowl,
And let its fieriest drop inflame the soul,
Which watches lonely as springs, cool and apart.

March 12, 1950
Chapel Hill

LIZARD

Reality? A lizard on a fence
Pants in the sun; the split pine-rail drips gum;
Over his beady eye the sky's immense.
Reality is here, throbbing and dumb.

Upon which actual scene our words intrude,
Speaking of hormones or the meddling State:
A tragic or a comic interlude.
The lizard in the great sun waits, will wait,

Ambassador of life base as our blood —
Baser, since all his heat's the sun's direct.
Reality? We've never understood,
Although we talk, cry havoc, and suspect.

April 22, 1951
Chapel Hill

ANDANTE CANTABILE

When, city-vexed, you pound the piano keys
Between a cigarette and cocktail, and
Whip up perniciously your chronic nerves
With bright self-pity, think of the drowsy land
We used to wander over, hand in hand.

O bless the memory of the summer fields,
The undulant ripe wheat that dreamed of bread,
The hum of bees building their honeycombs,
The towering cumulus, big with rain unshed;
And night, a starry canopy for your bed.

Rouse up the golden horns, timbrel and harp,
And celebrate the suns that shone above
The process of the flowering of those days
(The ablest music is not able enough)
When we possessed the dreaming earth, in love.

July 8, 1951
Chapel Hill

AFTER AN IMAGINED PAINTING
BY CEZANNE

The cards are shuffled and dealt out.
The players with their pipes and hats
Compose a still life richer than grapes.
The table's built of golden slats.

These fishermen (their nets hung out
Drying in zinnia-planted yards) —
One dwells upon their solid shapes,
The temporal wisdom of the cards.

The four apostles play it out.
The halo of their drifting smoke
Censers the game. Kings, queens, and knaves
Join forces with the little folk

Against each other. In or out?
Only the solid friendly four,
Who've fished all weathers and all capes,
Are certain, and listen toward the door.

September 1, 1952
Frederica

I STEPPED OUT

I stepped out of the dark house and the sky took off
  my head
And filled me with windy blueness and puddles that
  doubled the sky,
And my feet went over the addled bricks through patches
  of sun and shade
As if the whole wide world was moving, and not I.

The men in their fishermen's caps with their lewd jokes in
  the sun,
The girl with the warm round thighs, the brisk drip of the
  drain,
The tin roofs and the white sharp steeple and the wash on
  the line were one,
And the woman who hung the flapping wash out, and the
  jumping child in the lane.

O everything spoke together! Phrase after brilliant phrase
Was fit and in place and perfect and running over with joy,
And the clambering bean-vines were green and the
  morning-glories sang praise
And heaven gossiped with earth as when David was a boy.

I stepped out of the dark house and the sky took off
   my head
And when I came back in there was morning on ceiling and
   floor,
And everything was translated, was living that had been
   dead,
And I opened the closed windows, and left open the open
   door.

August 6, 1954
Frederica

THE CASTLE OF OTRANTO

My father's mansion is a ruined tower
Empty of terror, like a broken bell
Empty of music. Once it clanged with power
And had trap doors that opened down to hell,

And black ancestral armor that could speak
At midnight with a clapping jaw and groan
Of murders long committed. Knees grew weak
Climbing the winding stairs of sullen stone.

All's utterly changed. The terrible beauty, too;
The staring saints, the flaming ranks of heaven.
The bell's unrung where hosts of angels flew;
Obscenities chalk the wall where God was graven.

March 30, 1955
Chapel Hill

A SONG SASSETTA TAUGHT ME

The mystery of revelation
Is darker than the noonday sun,
The brightness of the hidden one
Is oddity and hesitation.
Not many can stand up and stare
The virgin blueness from the air.

I asked a wise man from the East
Upon an oriental beast,
Accompanied by a flight of cranes.
Arrayed in gold and antique signs,
He looked expert in deep designs.
But I got little for my pains.

How shall we formulate our yearning?
The years and centuries come and vanish.
The candles of the stars are burning,
Burning and burning to the socket.
Scholars begin and never finish
The *magnum opus* of their wisdom.

I lock your beauty in a locket
And dangle it by a silver chain
Of cold and continually dropping rain
Above the whale-boats of Nantucket.
The harbor lights confuse the issue,
But ignorance is as good as learning.

December 26, 1955
Chapel Hill

LOST

Peacocks and moths, gray-green lichen rings
On stone-gray stones, a shifting pattern of shadows.
Bird song was everywhere, lost in the shadows.
Their feathers drifted down. We drifted among old things.

Our widening circles were not wide enough
To carry us out of magic into newness,
Or even the familiar. There was a strangeness
In the spots of sunlight, in the stones' roughness.

I did not know how it was we had come there.
A choice we had made? I could not remember —
That, or the way in, or the wood's beginning.
I was there, and puzzled. You whispered, "There's nothing
    to fear!"

However, I was afraid. Once, by starlight,
I had thought that I perceived a hunter
Gliding just before or behind us, a black hunter
With white dogs on a leash. Were we his quarry?

I told myself we did not wish to leave,
That we were enchanted and could not even fancy
A more charming world, could not begin to fashion,
Even in words, a world we'd rather have.

But *was* it the glint of an arrow that headed us off?
That kept us circling, turning and returning
To earlier footsteps, to irrecoverable mornings?
We were lost, really. Not simply enchanted. Lost.

August 19, 1956
Frederica

THE LEADEN KEY

"Rebuild, rebuild the house," the dream seemed saying.
So I drove in a nail or two, an old bent lady
Offering guidance, holding the nails steady
Under the owner's gaze. The work was like playing.

Yet much was unpleasant. The boards I nailed were
   decaying,
The nails were slivers of rust. And something was shady
About the back stairs, the secret disordered study
Which I had peeped at before in my guilty straying.

The dream has a leaden key. I had been kissing
A young girl with dark hair, pretty and slender,
Unknown, a stranger, someone nameless and missing,

Whose face was blurred by the dark where I had caught her.
And then I knew, beneath the disguise, the tender
Death-vanquished, mourned-for lips of my own daughter.

June 3, 1958
Woods Hole

43

FIREWALKER

A boulder rose-burdened wall,
Black-mottled and dun,
Assumes, where the seagulls call,
The full weight of the sun.
I feel on my own back fall
The sea-burning sun.

I am no rampart of rock,
And my roses have shed
Their purple petals *en bloc*.
My sweet girl is dead.
Life reels with the shock.
Am I living or dead?

Yet the sun that rests on the wall
Rests also on me,
And me the seagulls call
To face, like the rocks, the sea:
To know my girl standing tall
On the burning sea!

June 6, 1958
Woods Hole

JACOB'S LADDER

The wind has skimmed the gray scum off the sky.
It is as blue and wide now as an angel's eye.
The swordfish weathervane on the church steeple
Points steadily northwest. At last the maple
That has for two days strained with every leaf
Stands like the Tree of Knowledge before the Thief.

I have no talent, am no William Blake,
Not even a Gulley Jimson splashing lake
And arsenic green and cobalt with a rope's end
On a twenty-foot spread of canvas. But I can ascend
By splintery rungs of prayer up Jacob's Ladder
And see the world as it was before the Adder.

Up Jacob's Ladder! A snapshot flashes there:
Me, playing a recorder over a girl's hair,
A four-year-old, as confident in my lap
As in the Almighty's. Doubtless the silver tap-
Tap-tap of my wandering fingers on the recorder
Was stumbling to find that tune so made to order

For a beginning woodwind: We ARE! climbING!
JaCOB'S! ladDER! Slowly. Slowly. The timing
Is important. — And she there, relaxed
Against my chest, under the woodwind, taxed
Me with no fault, no weakness. I was the Rock
From which the sweet music sprang at four o'clock.

Too much of luck and Eden! It could not last.
Time and the fall of Adam sent a blast
That ripped the woodwind out and broke my teeth
And carried the girl away and left a wreath,
And left a desert where my shadow alone
Crawled lame and small and ashamed on the sunstruck
    stone.

And I am still ashamed my shadow exists
Here where the lovely trees and creeping mists
Have clothed the stone with mercy. In despair
I climb three rungs, or less, up the ladder of prayer.
Under the angel's calm blue pitiless eye
I climb three rungs, or less, and fall with a sigh.

June 18, 1958
Woods Hole

MORNING

Next to our windows, in the tall grass
Dotted with daisies and a few irises,
Two slender trees, as the days pass,
Unfold their secrets and their silences.

We linger at breakfast to watch the small birds
Bend down the foliage with their hovering
(So tender it is), and we grope for words
To match the delicacy of the trees' flowering.

Their gracious bending and their pale greenness
Compose an airy heaven, their flowers hail us
With a salutation of exquisite sweetness;
And we prepare to take up our lives again, though our
    hearts fail us.

June 21, 1958
Woods Hole

AT NOBSKA

Sea-tumble, under the sea-ploughing wind,
Green, blue, blue-green, amethyst, white,
Snow-snarl over the pig-backed rocks;
And the terns plunging; and the long, low, hazy-finned
Blue islands, and the clear ascending height
Of the sky; and I, here where the surf knocks,

Contemplating — not, by any means, the face of man,
Or any work of man's, or any delight
Comprehensible by man, or any power
Within the control of man, no, but merely — a man's span
Of the infinite ingenuity of the supreme Light,
A jot of the Logos, a split-second of the towering

Billions of light-years of God's artifice!
Yet even the hairs of my head are numbered, and the fall
Of a single sparrow is noticed, and the diving tern
And the captured fish, and every blow and kiss,
Bounding or broken heart, slapped kelp, spray, star, all,
Inconceivably conceived by Him, are His minute concern.

August 9, 1958
Woods Hole

48

ROUNDING THE CORNER AT SCHOOL STREET

Under a black umbrella cutting a gray sky
By a gray-granite wall, I meet eye-to-eye
A fabulous pride of rose chrysanthemums,
A mass of pungent, dense, Van Gogh poems
Heavy with rain among their scalloped leaves
(Jungle of whorled suns in matte green sheaves)
To which a fly, green as a bottle, clings,
With brick-red eyes, and permits me to touch its wings.
That moment of contact restores from a dull
Forgottenness a young charcoal-speckled gull
That on the jetty yesterday charmed us by
Letting the children come near and not tensing to fly.
Slapped in, then, like a vibrant spot of paint,
Or a single yellow chrysanthemum, is a quaint
Quite real and quite unbelievable child, whose underlip
Last night in my dream was gold as a buttercup;
A gold-lipped, dreamed-of Chrysostomos,
Sent among gulls and chrysanthemums to pray for us.

August 26, 1958
Woods Hole

49

THERE WHERE I HAVE NOT COME

There where I have not come but have in mirrors
A moment looked, when morning broke over my shoulder
Or crickets chirped in the September grass
And the light fell through a side window on the paper
Where I was trying a poem — though no poem
Can equal what I intend: there where I have not come
Is all I can ever desire.

In that pure atmosphere the light is green,
Filtered through air like water, through foliage like flakes
Of sea-green jasper cut by a master workman
(The hills are bluish, the lakes are bluish-green),
And friends approaching down the long avenues,
Under the motion of leaves, are seen clearly,
As sea-bathers under water when the sun is high
And the waver of gold is upon them which the waves make.

There is no haste there, though the speed of thought
Is everywhere actual. Each one lovingly dwells
On the least gesture or inflection of voice,
For each one is a lover and rejoices
In all the motions of life, from leaf's to hand's,
From flower-like hand to hand-cut jasper leaf;
And all is calm there with fullness of thoughtful being,
And every perception is a lover's kiss.

September 5, 1959
Frederica

MICHELANGELO, OLD, WITH A SYMBOL
OF THE REDEEMER

A mood of world-weariness and religious devotion marked the old age of Michelangelo. In the following poem he is imagined as contemplating a luminous crystal, a lapis angularis, such as the old alchemists dreamed of acquiring, symbolic of Christ as the stone the builders rejected. The glow from it lights up his hand and his worn face. Off in the distance, the sculptures of Lorenzo and Moses and Night fade into insignificance under the supernatural blaze of the Divine Light.

Between the blunt thumb and Adam-making finger
Of the old man, a royal crystal turns,
Clearer than water but of architecture
Strict as the laws of Euclid — turns and burns
Softly between the thumb and crooked finger.

Glow and pulsation of all throbbing colors
Beat through the planes and angles of the stone,
Light up the cupping palm, make long and tender
The harsh lines of the bending face, enthrone
Joy in the worn cathedral of the sculptor.

Joy burns and turns, chafing with gentle pivot
The chalky thumb, the paint-stained finger, glows
Warmer than rose-windows, softer than candles,
And passes the shadow of the broken nose
Like water-walking love into the darkness.

"A structure of pure fire is my Beloved,
His bones are beams of light, his joints are suns,
His flesh is radiant with transfiguring radiance,
From his tremendous wounds the rainbow runs
That rides upon all storms, in joy and mercy."

So muses the old man; and black Lorenzo,
Enraged great Moses, elemental Night,
Become a faint intaglio, fading, fading,
Under the pulsing of that ardent light,
While slowly the crystal turns and burns in turning.

September 17, 1959
Chapel Hill

AN ENCOUNTER

A silent mockingbird on a gray stone
Pierces me with his eye. Who, wintering here,
Rakes in his garden? What right have I shown
To share his silence and his winter fare
Of rose-hips and hedge-berries, or scratch up
With stiff black claws December's small debris?
In summer did I sing? On what rooftop
Did I, moonlighting fowl, make melody?

The answer is not obvious. He and I
Match silences, like silent rapiers crossed.
We stand up to each other, wing to wing.
Neither retreats, and neither one will try
To prove that, once upon a time, in spring,
A kind of singing gift was his, now lost.

February 16, 1970
Chapel Hill